Superstars
of the
LOS ANGELES
LAKERS

by Annabelle T. Martin

AMICUS HIGH INTEREST AMICUS INK

Amicus High Interest and Amicus Ink
are imprints of Amicus
P.O. Box 1329, Mankato, MN 56002
www.amicuspublishing.us

Library of Congress Cataloging-in-Publication Data
Martin, Annabelle T.
  Superstars of the Los Angeles Lakers / by Annabelle T. Martin.
      pages cm. -- (Pro sports superstars (NBA))
  Includes index.
  ISBN 978-1-60753-769-4 (library binding)
  ISBN 978-1-60753-868-4 (ebook)
  ISBN 978-1-68152-019-3 (paperback)
  1. Los Angeles Lakers (Basketball team)--History--Juvenile literature. 2.
Basketball players--United States--Biography--Juvenile literature. I. Title.
  GV885.52.L67M37 2015
  796.323'640979494--dc23
                              2014045261

Photo Credits: Gus Ruelas/AP Images, cover; Chris Pizzello/AP Images,
2, 21; Jae C. Hong/AP Images, 5; George Long/Sports Illustrated/Getty
Images, 6–7, 9, 10, 22; Jeff Shaw/AP Images, 13; Carol Francavilla/AP
Images, 14; Steve Lipofsky/Corbis, 17; Andrew D. Bernstein/NBAE/Getty
Images, 18

Produced for Amicus by The Peterson Publishing Company
and Red Line Editorial.

Designer Becky Daum
Printed in Malaysia

HC 10 9 8 7 6 5 4 3 2 1
PB 10 9 8 7 6 5 4 3 2 1

TABLE OF CONTENTS

MEET THE LOS ANGELES LAKERS

The Lakers started in Minneapolis, Minnesota. They later moved to Los Angeles, California. That was in 1960. The Lakers have won 16 **titles**. The team has had many stars. Here are some of the best.

ELGIN BAYLOR

Elgin Baylor is a legend. He did it all. He played defense. He passed to teammates. He hit shots. Baylor was **Rookie of the Year** in 1959.

JERRY WEST

Jerry West joined the team in 1960. He was a leader. He worked hard. West led the Lakers to their first title. That was in 1972. West is a legend.

West later became a Lakers manager.

WILT CHAMBERLAIN

Wilt Chamberlain was an all-time great. His shots were accurate. He grabbed **rebounds**. He helped the Lakers win the 1972 title.

MAGIC JOHNSON

Magic Johnson joined the team in 1979. Fans loved him. He was a great passer. He could toss the ball to teammates behind his back. He also scored and grabbed rebounds.

KAREEM ABDUL-JABBAR

Kareem Abdul-Jabbar stands more than seven feet tall. He scored and **blocked** shots. Abdul-Jabbar won six **MVP** awards. He led the Lakers to five titles. The first was in 1980.

Abdul-Jabbar scored the most points in NBA history.

JAMES WORTHY

James Worthy **slam dunked**. He hit tough shots. He was called Big Game James. Worthy played great in playoff games.

The Lakers retired Worthy's jersey number, 42, in 1995.

18

SHAQUILLE O'NEAL

Shaquille O'Neal was powerful. He blocked shots. He grabbed rebounds. He helped win three titles in a row. The last was in 2002.

O'Neal had many nicknames. Many people just called him Shaq.

KOBE BRYANT

Kobe Bryant joined the Lakers after high school. He quickly became a star. He is a great shooter. He scores from all over. Bryant was the 2008 MVP.

The Lakers have had many great superstars. Who will be next?

21

TEAM FAST FACTS

Founded: 1947

Home Arena: Staples Center in Los Angeles, California

Mascot: None

Leading Scorer: Kobe Bryant (32,482 points as of February 25, 2015)

NBA Championships: 16

Hall of Fame Players: 15, including Kareem Abdul-Jabbar, Elgin Baylor, Jerry West, and James Worthy

WORDS TO KNOW

blocked – stopped a ball from going in the basket

manager – a person in charge of a sports team

MVP – Most Valuable Player; an honor given to the best player in the NBA each season

rebound – a ball that bounces away from the basket after a missed shot

retire a number – to honor a former player by not letting anyone else on the team use his jersey number

Rookie of the Year – an award given to the best new player in the NBA

slam dunked – made a shot in which the player jumps high and throws the ball down through the rim

title – an NBA championship victory

LEARN MORE

Books

Gilbert, Sara. *The Story of the Los Angeles Lakers*. Mankato, Minn.: Creative Education, 2011.

Kelley, K. C. *Los Angeles Lakers*. Mankato, Minn.: Child's World, 2013.

Websites

Los Angeles Lakers
http://www.nba.com/lakers
See videos of your favorite Lakers players.

NBA Hoop Troop
http://www.nbahooptroop.com
Follow your favorite basketball teams. Learn more about today's superstars.

INDEX